W9-AVB-440

MY FIRST LOOK AT COMMUNITIES

When the sun sets, city lights come on

A City

VALERIE BODDEN

CREATIVE EDUCATION

Published by Creative Education

P.O. Box 227, Mankato, Minnesota 56002

Creative Education is an imprint of The Creative Company

Designed by Rita Marshall

Photographs by Getty Images (amana images, Lonely Planet, National Geographic,

Photographer's Choice, Stone, Taxi)

Copyright © 2008 Creative Education

Printed in the United States of America

Library of Congress Cataloging-in-Publication Data

Bodden, Valerie. A city / by Valerie Bodden.

p. cm. — (My first look at communities)

Includes index.

ISBN-13: 978-1-58341-512-2

1. Cities and towns—Juvenile literature. 2. City and town life—Juvenile literature. I. Title.

HT 152.B63 2007   307.76—dc22   2006019353

First edition 9 8 7 6 5 4 3 2 1

A City

A BUSY PLACE!

A city is a busy place. It is full of all kinds of sights and sounds. People walk down the sidewalks. Traffic lights change colors. Car horns beep. Dogs bark.

Most cities are big. There are lots of buildings in cities. Some cities have very tall buildings. They are called skyscrapers. They look like they can touch the sky!

BIG CITIES HAVE HUNDREDS OF SKYSCRAPERS

There are smaller buildings in cities, too. Some are houses. Others are churches or grocery stores.

There are cities all around the world. Some cities are near the ocean. Other cities have a river running through them. Some cities are even in hot, dry deserts!

The Sears Tower in Chicago
is the tallest skyscraper in the
United States. It is 110 stories high!

THE TALL, BLACK SEARS TOWER HAS OFFICES INSIDE

CITIES ARE FILLED WITH COLORFUL LIGHTS AND SIGNS

CITY PEOPLE

Lots of people live in cities. Some people live in houses. Other people live in **apartments**. People in cities usually live close to each other. Most do not have very big yards.

Grown-ups in cities do all kinds of jobs. Some work in stores. Others work in big office buildings. Some people make things in **factories**. Some work in banks. Kids in cities go to school.

New York is called "the city
that never sleeps." That is
because it is busy night and day.

People who live in cities get around in lots of ways. Some people walk. Other people drive cars. Some people take a bus or a train. Some ride in **taxis**.

City Animals

There are lots of animals in cities. Some of the animals are pets. They live with people. Cats and small dogs are good city pets. So are fish.

In some cities, people ride

on underground trains.

These are called subways.

CITY DOGS NEED FRESH AIR AND EXERCISE

Other animals in cities are not pets. They live on their own. Mice and rats live in some cities. So do squirrels. There are lots of birds in cities, too. Pigeons are birds. They live in lots of cities.

Many cities have zoos. There are all kinds of animals at a zoo. You can see monkeys and zebras at a zoo. Elephants live in zoos, too. Some city zoos even have lions!

GIRAFFES LIVE IN MANY CITY ZOOS

Lots to Do

There are lots of things to do in cities. Cities have lots of stores to shop in. There are all kinds of restaurants to eat at, too.

Some cities have lots of **museums**. Some have big arenas where people can watch sporting events such as basketball games. Lots of cities have big parks where people can play or have picnics.

Toronto is the biggest city
in Canada. It has a castle
that people can visit!

There are even things to do in cities at night. You can watch a play or a concert. You can look at the pretty lights in the city's buildings. And you can think about what a fun place a city is, day or night!

NIGHTTIME DOES NOT SLOW DOWN CITY LIFE

Hands-on: Build a Skyscraper

Skyscrapers can be found in many cities. You can build your own skyscraper to play with!

What You Need

A small cardboard box

A medium cardboard box

A large cardboard box

Packaging tape

Crayons

What You Do

1. Tape each of the boxes shut with packaging tape.
2. Stack the medium-sized box on top of the large box. Stack the small box on top of the medium-sized box.
3. Draw a door near the bottom of the large box.
4. Draw windows on all of the boxes. Skyscrapers have lots of windows!
5. Imagine all of the people going into your skyscraper!

MANY SKYSCRAPERS LOOK OUT OVER CITY PARKS

Index

Words to Know

apartments—sets of rooms inside a bigger building with many others that look the same

factories—places where people make things such as cars, toasters, or crayons

museums—places where paintings or other important things are kept and shown

taxis—cars that people pay to ride in

Read More

Heywood, Rosie. *The Great City Search*. Tulsa, Okla.: Educational Development Corporation, 2005.

Hunter, Ryan Ann. *Into the Sky*. New York: Holiday House, 1998.

Roop, Peter, and Connie Roop. *A City Album*. Des Plaines, Ill.: Heinemann Library, 1998.

Explore the Web

The City: English-Spanish Picture Dictionary
http://www.enchantedlearning.com/languages/spanish/subjects/city.shtml

Welcome to the City http://www.harcourtschool.com/activity/cities

World Almanac for Kids http://www.worldalmanacforkids.com/explore/population2.html